Things I Wish I Could Tell You

by Casanova Green

Previously Published Works

Churching the Poem- Blue Mountain Review

Lancaster Nights- Frederickburg Literay and Art Review

Driving in an Ohio Winter- Sanctuary 2018: The Interdisciplinary Arts Magazine of Reinhardt University

Letter to my Unborn Child- The Blue Mountain Review

Letter to the Evangelical Church- Frederickburg Literay and Art Review

Student Teacher Conference I (titled as Student Teacher Conference) Sanctuary 2017: The Interdisciplinary Arts Magazine of Reinhardt University

The Score- Blue Mountain Review

Unpacking the Journey (Prologue)- Frederickburg Literay and Art Review

Writing with a Toddler- The Raw Art Review

Hard Reset- Blue Mountain Review

Things I Wish I Could Tell You

poems by: Casanova Green

Southern Collective Experience

www.southerncollectiveexperience.com

Copyright © 2021 by Casanova Green

All rights reserved. No part of this book may be reproduced or transmitted in any form or by any means, electronic or mechanical, including photocopying, recording, or any information storage and retrieval system, without permission in writing from the publisher.

ISBN: 978-1-7362306-0-2 – Paperback

Printed in the United States of America

This paper meets the requirements of ANSI/NISO Z39.48-1992 (Permanence of Paper)

Cover Design by Kaitlyn Young

Photography by Daniel Edeke

Table of Contents

Unpacking the Journey..*vii*

Family Album
    Lessons from Ms. Vera's Porch..1
    Notes..3
    Letter to My Father on his 55th Birthday..............................4
    Mirror...5
    Letter to My Unborn Child..6
    The Stars Applauded..7
    Daddy's Home..8
    Writing with a Toddler...9

Glory Carriers
    Controlled Burn..13
    Behold, I Do a New Thing...14
    Connect the Dots..15
    Letter to the Evangelical Church...16
    Letter to the Young Believers..17
    See-Saws and Catapults..18
    Churching the Poem...19
    Hard Reset..20
    Modern Day Lord's Prayer..21

Things I Wish I Could Tell You

    Urban Teacher's Playlist...25

    Student-Teacher Conference I..26

    Student Teacher Conference II...27

    Driving in an Ohio Winter..28

    Lancaster Sunset..29

    Lancaster Nights..30

    Reflections from 4'33"..31

    The Dry Season..32

    Tongue Tied...33

    Ambien Does Not Cause Racism..34

    The Score...35

Blurbs..37

Connect...39

Unpacking the Journey (Prologue)

Attention carpetbaggers and muckrakers,
tea-spillers and gossip pundits:
I have some dirty laundry to tell you.

Stinking piles of rags
vacuum-sealed for years
until crap piled flat and low.
Yet, I really needed one shirt—
the white button down
covered in black curvy script—
tucked away in God knows where.

The bag ripping began, and I found
pain plastered pastels,
gray-faded rainbow sneakers,
hats abused and misfolded,
wrinkled dreams
still tagged from the store,
and an amalgam of delicate experiences
that need gentle cleaning
knotted in moldy moments
because I refused to spring clean.

It became too much
too overwhelming
rifling through
the messy monsters
and ugly patterns
thirty years accumulated.

So join me Christian cowards,
staunch hypocrites,
broken deplorables,
and the judges dreading
justice's double-edged sword.
Watch me unpack

and make room for more.

Family Album

Family Album

Lessons from Ms. Vera's Porch

For my grandmother

Sultry Ohio summer humidity sulks
on inner-city streets as we sit
sheltered under your front porch.
Wasps buzz eavesdropping
into our silent conversation.

Your soft, strong arms rest comfortably
in the extra wide sleeves
of your handmade housedress
and hands rest on your stomach
as your aged brown skin marinates
and embraces this heat.
It reminds you of Alabama,
the farm, home.
Your light brown eyes turn hazel
when the sun hits your glasses
and you smile your sneaky grin
like you have a secret to tell.

We sip our red drink
and stare at the collard greens between us.
In this searing heat, we walked
to the other side of the neighborhood
across from the church and the factory
to a junk-filled red house
with an outdoor rusted car museum
and you saw these collards
so small the gopher you hate
won't give them a first glance
and saved them.

They sit between us
lapping up blue miracle water
thirsting to grow.
You take a swig of your drink,
smack your reddened lips,
and look right at me:
"Cas, you see they ain't got no love."

You hold the greens and their glass
in the palm of your soft wrinkled hands
and point at it with the other.
"Now y'all listen here. I got you away
from them evil folk down the street.
I'm your momma now and I love you.
You hear me, greens? I love you.
Now I need you to grow."

A couple days later,
we sit in the same searing heat.
Me. You. Greens. Miracle water.
A person from the neighborhood
comes over and says hello.
Withered and limped by life,
a woman of thirty whose life
sagged her to sixty
Hair spiked and broken at the edges
with the rest in a small bun and
disheveled clothing.

You give me that glance
as she drags herself up the walk.
Your grin comes back:
"Cas, you see she ain't got no love."

You fold your soft wrinkled hands
and hear her story for the week
that you've heard eight times already.
Finally having a moment to speak,
you point to her and say
"Now listen here. I got you away
from them evil folk down the street.
I'm your momma now and I love you.
You hear me? I love you.
Now I need you to grow."

Notes

In memory of my mother

I remember the look in your eyes.
The look of "I want to be there."
You have achieved your goal
to see me graduate college.

Behind your mahogany eyes,
the dark knells ring
of sunset.

You smile then kiss my cheek.
The smell of White Diamonds
whiffs from your chestnut skin
and your voice,
raspy from scratching out your last strains
of earth-bound melody
whispers, "I love you."

I didn't know your song
would be our last.
I didn't know you were
one week away from relief.
I didn't know my last memory
would be your radiant face.

Letter to My Father on his 55th Birthday

You were invisible to me once,
a passing breeze chilling me
out of the warmth of love
to the edge of the Antarctic
guarded by glaciers built
by empty promises,
frozen by your passing presence.

One day, much older,
I looked at the man you became
and saw me-
over worked, overburdened
by needs not met,
dreams restlessly packed
with secondhand problems
you were forced to carry alone.

I pitied you.
I finally heard
the constant apologies,
understood the late nights,
and reconciled the times
you thought money equaled happiness.
The fearful child in me
finally felt safe.
I loved you again.

I apologize for neglecting you,
not forgiving your youthful fears
of fatherhood.
Your fresh-fired love
has melted my metal heart
refining me to love you again.

Mirror

for my Butterfly

I found you years ago
glistening like clear diamonds
wrapped in sterling silver.
I saw my reflection in you that night
but you only saw a windowed mirage.
We began our reflective quests
and each time we thought
we found our reflection,
each was a funhouse distortion.

Rather than believe
the rock-hard lies hurled
by lovers who tarnished our value
or allow the mildew
of past actions unearned
to dig deep and destroy
the Godly love that we reciprocate,
we let the quest, the dust,
the choking chemical abrasives
prepare us for now, for this.

Now I when I see you, I see me.
When I hear you, I hear me.
When I need to be polished,
you make me shine
and I make you gleam
when the world wants to
streak you with gloom.

Letter to My Unborn Child

We picked names for you as we coasted through
the palmetto-lined highways of the Carolinas
heading to our delayed honeymoon.

We returned home and you were our surprise.
Your mother was told she could not have children.
I honestly thought my health would prevent you from happening.

We shared with those closest to us.
We even saw a grainy picture of you
as the doctor confirmed you were real.

I stared at your mother laying helpless
whispering penitent apologies
as I looked at the bleak spring Lancaster twilight.

My mind began to wander.
I asked God why he took you.
Heaven was silent.

I whispered "I'm not mad at you. I love you."
We held hands for minutes that seemed like days
as we realized you were a fading memory.

We said "And we know that all things
Work together for the good of them who
Love God and are called according to his purpose."

I picture you looking at me
with your large gray eyes, olive-toned skin,
and your mother's wide smile.

I touch your brown woolen hair and wonder
if you would want dreadlocks like me
or let your hair fall like willow branches.

I hold and caress you and sing the latest song I wrote.
The vibrations of the notes and the heaving of my chest
Lull you into a peaceful rest.

I love you, my precious child.

The Stars Applauded

Outside Hill Freeman Library
2016

The stars come out this night in purest white.
An audience of thousands who come
to see a show called Life on Earth.
I walk barefoot from one building to another
slowly becoming aggravated
with Georgia's sweet sticky heat. Realizing the time,
I pick up the phone and dial my wife.

She answers the phone in Ohio.
The stars turn their heads northward
to see her face as I begin to talk.

"Hello, love"

"So, don't get mad at me."

"Why would I get mad at you?"

"We're pregnant."

The stars look down to see my face
white with fear but red with excitement.
Holding back tears, I ignore the bug bites
and the high humidity and just say
"Okay."

Daddy's Home

I drag my day behind me
sopping heaviness
as I carry groceries in the house
muffling rustles
as you and your mother sleep.

I kiss her forehead
and glance in your direction.
Thank God—
still sleeping.
But you're playing possum
and horn puppy whimpers
and muffled mmm's
until I walk towards you
with a half-off coat
and your pillared smile grows
joined with flailing arms and legs
until I come to you.

To you, my hard day means nothing
and my hour-long drive home
is not a concern.
You look past my wizened face
and see daddy's home
and you are safe.

Writing with a Toddler

Biting your little lower lip,
you scoot, left leg extended,
brow scrunched, chasing after
the ball I threw
because you reclined housecat-style
on my journal
when I was in mid-thought.

You come back to the couch ballless
yet just as determined to climb
on the couch next to me
murmuring and horning,
grasping until you make it.

As you walk across the sectional,
you stop to read these words.
They look nothing
like an old lady rabbit
telling a baby rabbit
to quit saying good night
or a group of snugglesauri.

You climb down again
to find your next mission,
your next game,
until you see me
scribble words again.

Glory Carriers

"To understand the glory of God, you must understand his nature. The only way to understand his nature is authentic relationship."

Controlled Burn

You were my safety.
I would climb in you
and navigate the lines
between shame and euphoria.
You were beautiful,
a diamond hidden in coal
waiting under pressure
for me to find your value.

But now, I've realized
I've outgrown you.
Your secrecy cannot contain
the passionate power
which is deep in me.
You were my secret cave
that become my abysmal prison.
We are Clark Kent and kryptonite
and only the sun can save me from you.

So I must set you on fire.
If I keep you around,
I will always come back
for a Hell-bound pilgrimage.
I must let Heaven's blaze
burn me and you
until I am refined
and you are an ashen memory.

Behold, I Do a New Thing

A woman's prayerful wails fill
the air of my office, the haunting beauty
of holy travail prepares me for my next task.
A month ago, I was listening to this same song
but sitting in a different office with matted carpet
instead of shining wood linoleum and the walls
a mundane tan instead of dancing gray
and vibrant green. The mesmerizing fragrance
of frankensenced anointing oil
no longer dances across my nose.
Only the stench of despair and dereliction
marches loudly down the dark halls of the building.

Behold, I do a new thing...

The multicolored paintings,
so foreign in the old office,
reside comfortably on new walls
like they knew they would end up here.
I am the black of the rainbow room
the white outcasts and the prism others.
But they fail to see that my blackness
is a merging of everything they want.
I wait and wonder in this rickety chair
finding my place, finding me.

Behold, I do a new thing...

The weight of jealous bondage
sags on my shoulder like sandbags
prepared for a flood.
Golden carrot promises dangle
before my eyes but I know
I am not a donkey towing the line.
My fingers dance on the desk impatiently
like a student waiting for the teacher's attention
but there is only a whisper...

Behold, I do a new thing.

Connect the Dots

Pixel by pixel, we build the image.
From miniscule whispers,
we mosaic the world.
But perception shuffles our screen
so we see what we want to see.
Each image is a larger blip
of the show God watches
from his throne room
threaded together
into a flawed monster.

Letter to the Evangelical Church

You have cried for revival
begging God for a voice
to speak your truth.
I hope you're happy.

I hope you see your hive mentality—
busy bees buzzing around stinging
because you are caught up in smelling flowers
instead of saving souls.
But you fail to realize
you are in danger of
Colony Collapse Syndrome.

I pray that you step out
of your privilege and realize
your brown and yellow friends
are afraid of what happens next-
Will their churches and homes be firebombed?
Will they get deported?
Will we return to the times of Jim Crow?

It's time to live up to your name:
evangelize, carry the light
burning blue hot and strong
to the shadows just beyond
megachurch lots and Sunday pews
where the Savior's crimson love
still runs strong and
where the lowly loves of God live.

Letter to the Young Believers

Wide-eyed wunderkinds seeking
to be loved hard by fathers and mothers
yet are afraid to face the fact
that freedom has a price,
please realize the worth
of priceless intimacy.

Riding the choppy waves
of this religious relational experience
requires being beautiful habitations
of the God that is more
than a Sunday song
or a Wednesday study.
He desires to dig deep
and commune with you,
feet propped,
and speak hidden truth to you.

He is not concerned with stages and lights
but corner tables and conversations
which cause the lowest man
to gain greater strength.
Nor is He moved by superhero feats
of fiery tongues or arrow-accurate prophecy
not seasoned or dipped in his blood-shed love.

So don't let the kaleidoscope lights
and strange choking hazes fool you
or the enticing words of broken men
lure you to shards.
He wants you to know His love inside out
and sit with you at His sprawling table.

See-Saws and Catapults

What was once a fun game
is now a battle for life
as we bounce for balance.
You are too heavy
to carry and counter
and my legs are crying out
from the pain of constant rebounding.

Your mischief is showing strong.
Your spike eyes gleam
and your serpentine smirk slithers
as you take a bounding leap
praying I launch high and forward
and land on the thorny vines
tangled in unrelenting pain.

I brace and lay back
letting the launch
flip me back to Earth
to stand on stable ground again.

Churching the Poem

If I could put a Hammond B3
wailing hard and trumpeting
a ii-V-I backbeat behind these words,
I bet you that you would
stand and clap a syncopated beat
that tells me you're feeling something deep
or beat a blessing
into a Jesus praying hands tambourine
as the choir squalls and barks these lines.

If I could get a fire-baptized preacher
to whoop and holler these words
with neck veins pulsing,
sweating like Jesus in Gethsemane,
I know you would be
the three-piece suited deacon
walking up to him incredulously
hollering a baritoned "Preach, Doc!'
or the young soprano in her puffy robe
chirping "You better say that!"

If I could get a faith healer
to whisper these words
and then jolt you to Glory
with a gentle touch,
I know you would rest deep
as you're carried high
and come back to Earth
breathless in ecstatic wonder
tear-streaked and unburdened
by the cares of the world.

But this is merely a poem.
Yet it still prophecies and enlightens
the murky minds of men.
It doesn't need an organ
meanly tuned to A-flat
and imagery is the seven-piece band
playing fast,
walking up and down
twelve-tone chromatics.
The words don't need a growl or holler
to be knife-sharp or sniper-accurate
as they process pain, lecture love,
and change us all.

Hard Reset

I'm frozen again--
too overloaded from my life
to process the files of stress
and the anxiety applications
clogging my memory
stopping up the random access
of my present task.
I thought my software was safe
but a trojan horse rolled in
full of old thoughts and habits
and mucked up the motherboard.
No antivirus can tame it
and my firewalls are pocked
with cyber-frozen sledgehammer holes.
I have no choice but to submit--
go back to square one, factory reset.
Back to the old foundations,
a second chance to be right again.

Modern Day Lord's Prayer

Our Father, who art in Heaven,
hallowed be thy name.
Thy kingdom come, thy will be done
in Earth as it is in Heaven.
Give us this day our daily bread
and forgive us or debts
as we forgive our debtors.
Lead us not into temptation
but deliver us from evil
for thine is the kingdom, the power,
and glory forever, amen.

I've called you holy and provider.
I've asked for forgiveness and protection.
Yet in this moment of piercing silence
my heart and mind find these words
an empty mimic stuck in rigor
because my soul is clinging to life.

I feel unworthy of your daily grace
and I want my will to be done.
My thoughts ravage me
as my emotions tally the hurts,
the lies, the pain that hangs limp
on my heart's broad and broken shoulders.

Temptation pulls me left
while I want to be righteous
and I watch everyone
enjoy her cheap wine
drinking deep her fun
shouting "The world is ours."

In my frailty, here you sit strong
seeing beyond the cynicism
bred by abuse and pain.
You wash me with your words
and each fall down pure
and settles my doubt.

So, Daddy, Abba, sitting high in Heaven
yet resting next to me,
you are holy.
Let Heaven touch the Earth
and what you say be so
in all your creation.
Continue to supply my needs
and teach me how to forgive
and love like you.
Protect me from myself:
mistakes, cruelty, frailty.
Everything is yours
including me...
Amen.

Things I Wish I Could Tell You

Urban Teacher's Playlist

The cacophony of profanity condenses over my head as
    my hands clatter
these words like rain while TLC's "Waterfalls" plays

and a student unleashes a torrent of complaints
    and another
types harder and faster than I do as we attempt

to make our deadlines. Erykah Badu, fly me
    on a plane
and give me your window seat because I need

an escape, a get-away from the straight-jacket
that has become my life. You know, a beach

or an island away from Ohio's white-washed winter
and muddy confusion which is called Lancaster,

Missa Green, do I havta write dis poem?
    Yes, you have to do it.
But I don't know howta write no poem.

My soul shakes and turns cold as she continues her
    syncopated rapping
on the keyboard and I focus on this poem.

"I wanna scream and shout..." Yes, Britney I understand
    your once bald, crazed phase.
"It goes on and on and on and on..." And I wish
    it would stop.

Student-Teacher Conference I

The bittersweet scent of marijuana
wafts my nostrils as you slouch before me
disheveled and unkempt.
Your bloodshot eyes plead with me
for one more chance to make things right.

I see the damage
the hellhounds have done to you.
The mosaic of tattoos wandering down your arms
kissing your neck
covering the scars
of battles long fought against poverty.
The smell of cigarettes and alcohol
are the ether of attempts to numb
years of abuse and dejection.

Your icy persona melts as you fight
back tears because it is too painful
for you to share the reasons-
the addictions, the hyperactivity,
the lack of loving care,
the comfort with failure-
which bring us to this stalemate.

I give the usual speech:
try to be here as much as possible,
you are not an island,
do as much as you can,
I believe in you.
But the glass of your eyes reveals
I have lost you again.

Student Teacher Conference II

Am I high enough yet?
Am I flying above
the bullets that tagged
my ears but did not
move into my body
last night?

My stomach twists
because my last meal
was last night—
dry ramen—
because mom was too high
to pay the bill.

Now I have to sit across
from this man who looks like me
but doesn't know me
He doesn't care.
He doesn't want to see me
but I have to graduate.

I don't want to be like
my father who died
chasing a drug dream or
like my mom with a kid
before she should have a kid.
I can't be like my brothers
and sister stuck jobless
hoping someone will care for me.

He says the same thing every time
        try to be here as much as possible—
I have no car
and I work too late
        do as much as you can—
the only internet I have
is on my phone
        I believe in you—
No one else has
so I'll keep doing what I do
alone.

Driving in an Ohio Winter

As snow falls relentlessly
and blankets cold cotton
on the black and brown earth
remember these steps:

Take the freeways because
they are a mushy zone
pre-marinated for safe passage.

Clear sight is important,
wipe your headlight eyes
and make sure your wipers
do not streak your view.

Take your time
and drive the lowest gear
because steel snails survive
better than crushed beetles.

Black ice is a slippery seductress
hidden under brine mixtures
and pretzel-salted slush.
In case she grabs you,
drive into the skid
and let her whirl you until
jealous Newton forces her to stop.

Keep a double distance
and let the tracks ahead guide you.
They will never steer you wrong
and give a safe shell for the journey.

Be aware of the emergencies:
Level 1, slow yet cautious
Level 2, torrential blowing and trucks failing
Level 3, don't even try—

True love is worth it.

Lancaster Sunset

Ohio's indecisive March
arrhythmically gasps for hot air
while we ants scurry outside
for the last drops of early spring.
Winter creeps among early blossomed trees
loving them to wooden bone again.

My heart craves warmth
as the blue marbled day
deeply kisses the violet night's
red-orange sunset lips
and turns the sky cloudlessly dark
with night's white eye waxing,
and beauty marks twinkling.

Lancaster Nights

Dandelion seeds bob atop
clear cold summer night waters
and crickets chirp tonight's forecast—
clear, 62.
As I recline shallowed
in striped boxes
in a polka-dotted kiddie pool,
the stars gleam
over the Appalachia edge
I call home.

My body and the water
reach common temperature
as the solaced whispers
of near midnight winds
entice me to embrace
the peace of this moment.
But technology cuts in jealously
with choral ohms
of air conditioners.

How crudely I sit with pen and paper
scribbling enlightened thoughts in darkness
while my phone rests inches away
outside the waters silent.

Reflections from 4'33"

Distant cicadas maraca their lust
and sparrows solo their love ballads
as children squeal and horn their joy
tossing a ball back and forth.

The cicadas heighten their shaking
to drown out the overtoned droll
of freeways and urban sprawl.
Each crescendos and decrescendos
adding the occasional sforzando
alerting the other of its presence.

The Sun takes her nightly bow
and welcomes Sister Moon
to wax poetic and wane dramatic
as the stars come to hear
the silent prayers of dormant earth
rising towards heaven,
the innocent whisper wishes
given to nonexistent nebulas,
the panted promises
of passionate nights.

The Dry Season

This page is a white sand desert
frozen by potential's heat
waiting for inky rain
to blot and streak
until loquacious life springs up
from the pulpy underbelly.

The creator stares upon the sands
too afraid to cause imperfections
by creating another platypus nonsense
or rehashing the same Jabberwocky.

So he leaves it
blind-heated—
waiting.

Tongue Tied

1.
It's more than a frog...
There is no croak left to give,
I can't hop to it,
and my tongue has not lashes
to whip juicy flies to death.
I've bitten it too deep
only leaving a bloody stump
salty with the world
too iron-saturated to say anything
to soften lingual sword slashes.

2.
You all scream to me "Speak up!"
yet the snowy slope
is invaded by wasps
and it is too treacherous
to let out steel-edged truths
which ting avalanches
snowballing us to oblivious,
ignoring the whitened tumble
until we are face down
encased in heavy snow
sucking in ice
overtaken by the weight
of ill-timed explosions.

Ambien Does Not Cause Racism

Sleeping minds speak woke thoughts
and drunk minds shriek sober secrets,
but you can't blame the ether
for the reaction of the consumer.

It was the hydra hidden within you,
heads working separately together,
that tapped the little bluebird
to sing bleak notes
in seventy measures in common time.

We have grown tired of the balms
designed to hide the bigot side
and rather people just expose
their ugly truth up front
rather than let absinthe and elixirs
be the zebra that lures the lions.

The Score

What will history say
about us in twenty years?

Will we wave victory banners
high and coo watching
the long-departed soldier
clutch his bride, dipping her low,
kissing her deep in Times Square?

Will we be burnt shadows
on glowing rubbled walls
waiting for radiation
 to die decades after
we have vaporized
and those who remain
pray cancer kills quickly?

Will history before our present
be fact mashed murkily
into tasty fiction garnished with fear
while poems and art are lined black,
redacted and gagged, hushed
in place of newspeak?

Perhaps,
history will be gracious:
the Union will still stand.
I, greyed and wrinkled,
will write new words
and preach the same Gospel.
But the Republic,
for which it stands,
may be too divided, too fractured,
to handle the same heart
or the same name.

History, you unbiased judge,
take pity on our idiocy
and do not strike
the gavel yet.
There is too much
yet to be done
before the sentence begins.

Blurbs

Things I Wish I Could Tell You, heavy as the weight of everyday questions asked. Casanova Green, with keen eye and clear vision, pushes us beyond the surface dimensions of easy, everyday answers. Electric in places, subtle in its power in other places, always elegiac, these poems persistently remind us of that which reminds itself of each of us. Rendered in rhythm, this collection emotionally examines and attempts to explain the range: Home to work, home to school, home to church and back home again.

Earl S. Braggs, author of Negro Side of the Moon

Things I Wish I Could Tell You is a heartfelt and heartwarming book in which Casanova Green uses everything he knows of American vernacular and black storytelling. These poems tell like secrets. This is a book interested in forgiveness and salvation.

Jericho Brown, author of The Tradition
2020 Pulitzer Prize Winner, Poetry

Yes, you should read this book. But don't just read this book—speak it out loud, put it in your mouth, sing it if you have to, "beat a blessing / into a Jesus praying hands tambourine / as the choir squalls and barks these lines." In faith and in doubt, in harrow and in hallelujah, these poems come from a speaker who says things through his soul, who shakes his sentences till the verbs become hinges that make their own doors. Go through them!

Kathryn Cowles, author of Maps and Transcripts of the Ordinary World

Debut collections of poetry come and go every year. Unnoticed, most are forgotten; however, Things I Wish I Could Tell You will not be among the forgotten. This debut will resonate with poetry lovers because from the very beginning when Casanova Green shouts "Attention" to all the "carpetbaggers and muckrackers,/tea-spillers and gossip pundits:/I have some dirty laundry to tell you" what can you do except listen? Green is a young man who brings to life his mother's dream of seeing her son graduate college, yet the avatar of contemporary wisdom is also the angry son who writes an apology to his father, years later when he has an understanding of his father's burdensome life. To hold these poems is to hold a man's dreams, to savor them, because as in "Driving in an Ohio Winter," you must "Take your time/and drive the lowest gear. . . ." This is good advice on how to live life, a metaphor for reading this fine collection of poems, slowly, understanding that "True love is worth it" because you will fall in love with these poems. In the end, Casanova Green dazzles the reader with hope and the promise that "history will be gracious:/but not yet ready to cast judgment." The judgment here is this: what a wonderful debut.

William Walsh, author of Fly Fishing in Times Square

Connect

Currently, Casanova Green is the Owner of CGCreate, LLC and serves as the Lead Pastor of True Vision Christian Community headquartered in Lancaster, OH with outreaches and churches in South Carolina and India. He also works as the Journalism Program Manager at Hocking College. He and his family reside in Lancaster.

Casanova Green-

CGCreate, LLCWebsite: www.cgcreate.online
Facebook: cgcreatellc
Instagram: @casanovatlgreen
Email: casanovagreenmusic@gmail.com

True Vision Christian Community-

Giving: truevisionlancaster.org/giving
Facebook: truevisionlancaster
Instagram: @truevisionlancaster
Email: admin@truevisionlancaster.org

www.ingramcontent.com/pod-product-compliance
Lightning Source LLC
LaVergne TN
LVHW011900060526
838200LV00054B/4445

9 781736 230602